IF0251

Instructional Fair, Inc.

Getting Ready Kindergarten

Math

Reading

Science

Language

Social Studies

Spelling

Instructional Fair, Inc., Grand Rapids, MI

Getting Ready for Kindergarten

About the Book

This book is designed to review many of the concepts and skills addressed in pre-school, or possibly at home. Due to the level, parent involvement is a necessity. You will need to read the directions to your child before he/she can begin to work. In some cases you will read the directions as your child works.

One factor built into the book is the opportunity for your child to communicate verbally, which is an essential part of your child's development. Use every page to its fullest potential by talking about the pictures. Many times the directions will focus on a topic about which you and your child can converse. Don't limit yourselves to the topics. Feel free to expand or change the topic to focus on your child's interests. This will help to increase vocabulary, practice correct usage of verb forms, concentrate on speaking in complete sentences and even build self-confidence.

Some page themes may inspire a real-life, hands-on experience – such as making an ice-cream sundae. Hands-on experiences are a wonderful learning tool, especially for the young. See how many experiences you and your child can share!

About the Author

Renee Cummings is one of Instructional Fair's most accomplished authors. Renee holds a Bachelor's Degree in Elementary Education from Oregon State University. Her 18 years of teaching experience encompasses various elementary levels, as well as remedial reading.

Credits

Author: Renee Cummings
Illustrator: Cindy Adams
Project Director/Editor: Sue Sutton
Editors: Rhonda DeWaard, Sharon Kirkwood
Cover Graphics: Julie Wiley
Production: Pat Geasler

ISBN 0-88012-948-4   Printed in the USA   IF0251 Getting Ready for Kdg.

Table of Contents

Answer Key (in middle of book)

Getting Ready for Kindergarten

Write the child's name.
This book belongs to...

Write your name.

Address

Write the child's address on the lines. Have the child recite it.

Copy your address. Color the house the same color as your house.

Telephone Number

Write the child's telephone number. Then have him/her point to and say each number. Have him/her practice touching the telephone numbers on the telephone as they're said.

Copy your telephone number.

Self-Awareness

Discuss people's likenesses and differences and how every person is unique.

Draw a picture of yourself. Write your name.

This is me.

_____

_ _ _ _ _ _ _ _ _ _ _ _ _ _ _

_____
name

Small Motor Skills

Discuss what is happening in the picture.

Trace the dotted lines. Color the picture.

Small Motor Skills

Discuss make-believe and real pigs.

Trace the dotted line from the pig to the mud puddle.

MUD
PUDDLE

Small Motor Skills

Discuss mass transit systems used in big cities.

Draw a line through the streets from the train to the skyscrapers.

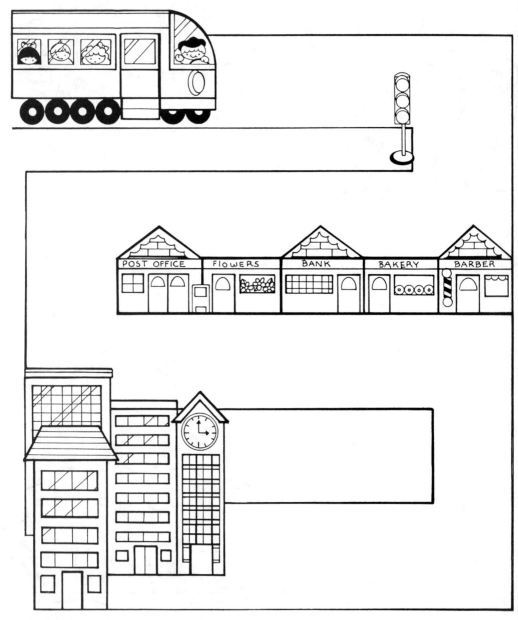

Discuss the child's favorite kinds of donuts.

Trace the dotted lines. Color the picture.

Small Motor Skills

Discuss oceans.

Trace the dotted line from the starfish to the rock.

Small Motor Skills

Discuss the picture.

Draw a line from the beaver to the dam following the path.

Small Motor Skills

Use with page 13.
Discuss make-believe and real dogs.

Small Motor SKills

As you read each color word, have the child pick the correct crayon to color in the box.

Color the boxes. Cut out the boxes and paste them in the cupboard shelves on page 12.

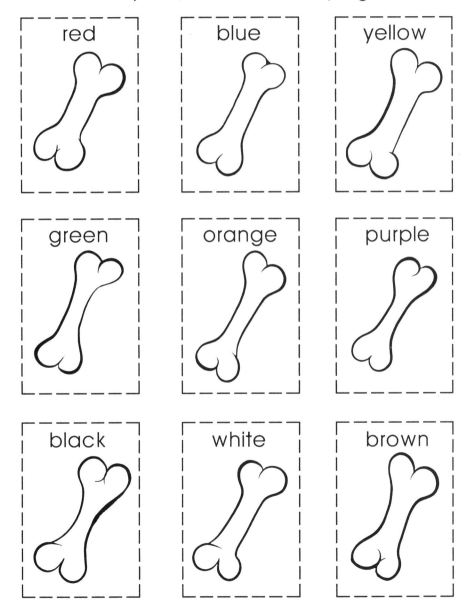

red

blue

yellow

green

orange

purple

black

white

brown

Classifying

Discuss the pictures.

Draw a circle around the things that you can wear.

Small Motor Skills

Use with page 17.
Discuss different types of cupcakes and how to make them.

Small Motor Skills

Use with page 16.
As you read each color word, have the child pick the correct
crayon to color the circle.

Color the circles. Cut out the circles and paste
them on the cupcake on page 16.

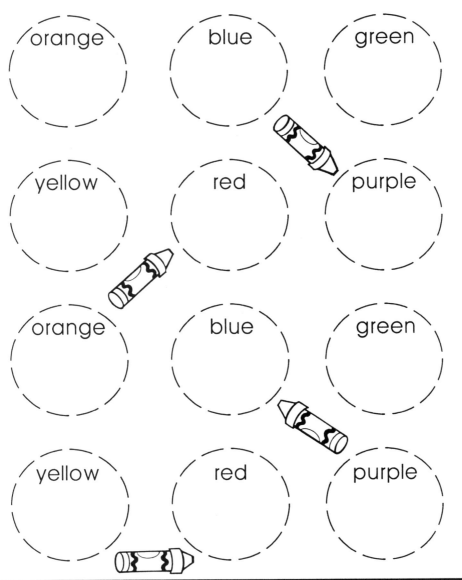

orange   blue   green

yellow   red   purple

orange   blue   green

yellow   red   purple

Visual Discrimination

Discuss getting ready for bedtime. Have the child describe the three pictures in each row.

Color the two pictures in each row that are the **same**.

Visual Discrimination

Discuss car racing.

Draw lines to match the cars that look the **same**.

Visual Discrimination

Discuss what you can put on crackers to make tasty snacks. Have the child describe the three pictures in each row.

Color the cracker in each row that is **different**.

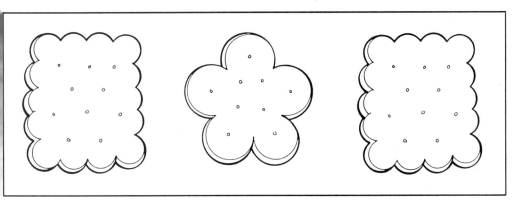

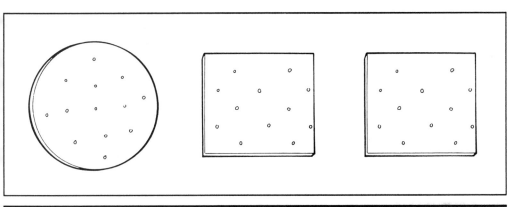

Visual Discrimination

Use with page 23.
Discuss favorite zoo animals.

Cut out the puzzle pieces on page 24. Paste
them where they belong in the puzzle frame.
Color the picture.

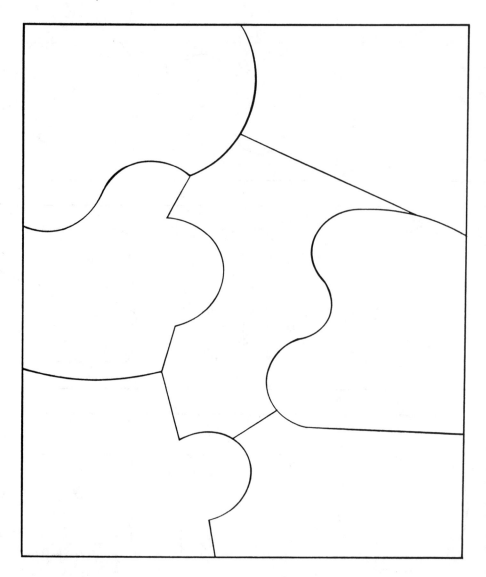

Visual Discrimination

Use with page 22.

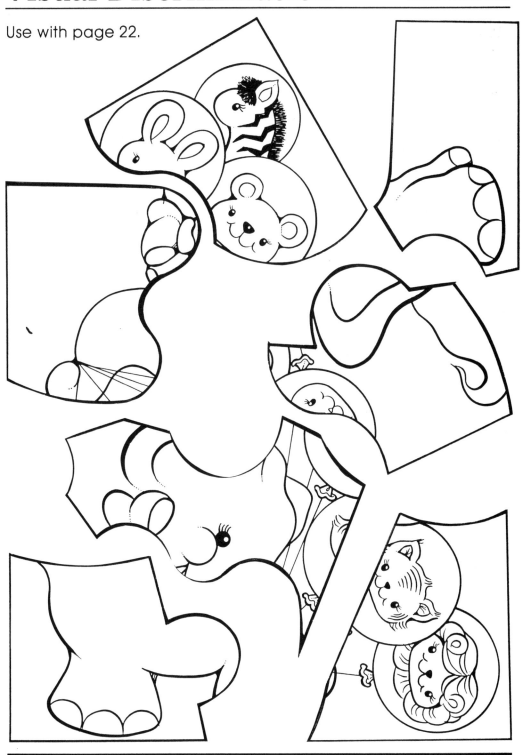

Visual Discrimination

Discuss the toys in the top picture.

Find and circle 8 things in the top picture that are not in the bottom one.

Have the child name all of the pictures.

Draw lines to match the pictures that begin with the **same** sound.

Auditory Discrimination

Have the child name all of the pictures.

Draw lines to match the pictures that begin with the **same** sound.

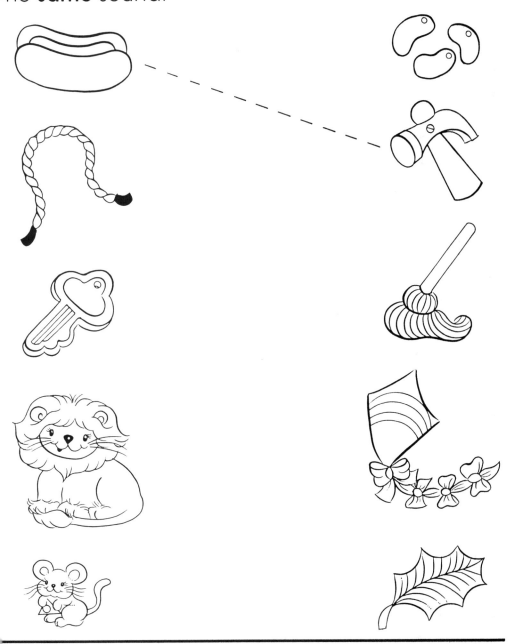

Auditory Discrimination

Have the child name all of the pictures.

Draw lines to match the pictures that begin with the **same** sound.

Auditory Discrimination

Have the child name all of the pictures.

Draw lines to match the pictures that begin with the **same** sound.

Reading Readiness

Have the child describe what is happening in each of the pictures.

Circle the picture in each row that shows what happened **first**.

Reading Readiness

Have the child describe what is happening in each of the pictures.

Circle the picture in each row that shows what happened **last**.

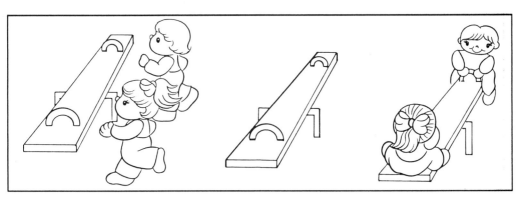

Alphabet

As you point to each letter, have the child name it.

Connect the puzzle dots in alphabetical order.

A B C D E F G H I J K L M N O P Q R S T U V W X Y Z

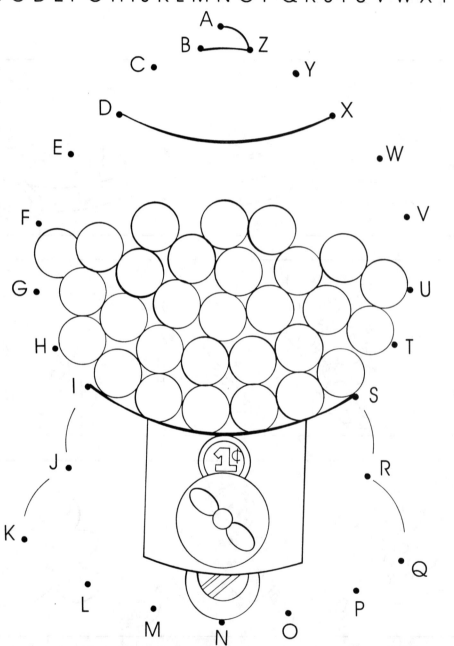

Alphabet

As you point to each letter, have the child name it.

Connect the puzzle dots in alphabetical order.
a b c d e f g h i j k l m n o p q r s t u v w x y z

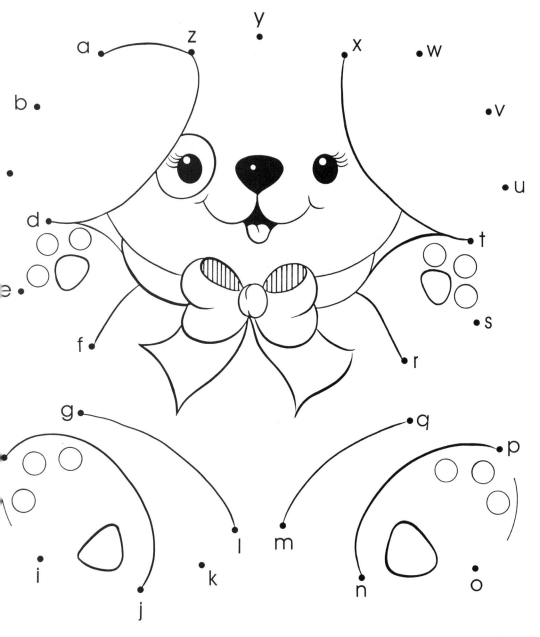

Colors

Have the child name things that are red.

Color the spaces marked **red** with a red crayon.

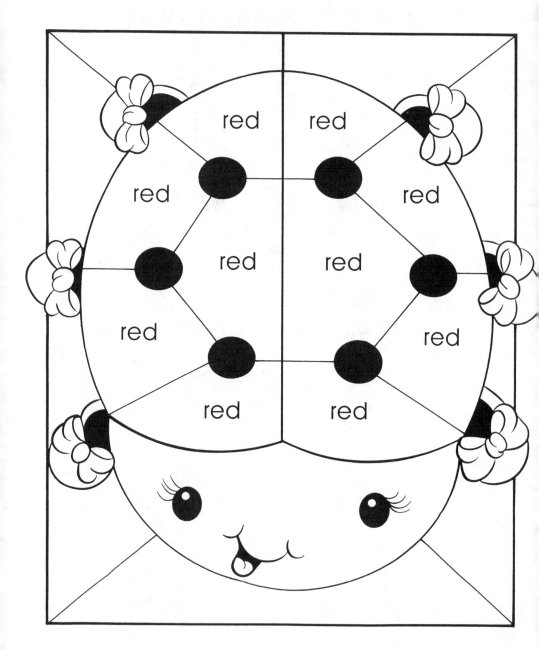

Colors

Have the child name the pictures and the color.

Draw a line from the crayon to the things that could be **blue**. Color the pictures.

Colors

Have the child name the pictures and the colors.

Color the paintbrush and the three pictures that could be **yellow**.

yellow

Answer Key

Getting Ready for Kindergarten

Write the child's name.
This book belongs to...

Answers will vary

Write your name.

©1993 Instructional Fair, Inc.   2   IF0251 Getting Ready for Kdg.

Address

Write the child's address on the lines. Have the child recite it.

Answers will vary

Copy your address. Color the house the same color as your house.

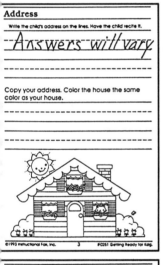

©1993 Instructional Fair, Inc.   3   IF0251 Getting Ready for Kdg.

Telephone Number

Write the child's telephone number. Then have him/her point to and say each number. Have him/her practice touching the telephone numbers on the telephone as they're said.

Answers will vary

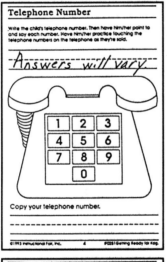

Copy your telephone number.

©1993 Instructional Fair, Inc.   4   IF0251 Getting Ready for Kdg.

Self-Awareness

Discuss people's likenesses and differences and how every person is unique.

Draw a picture of yourself. Write your name.

This is me.

Answers will vary.

name

©1993 Instructional Fair, Inc.   5   IF0251 Getting Ready for Kdg.

Small Motor Skills   tracing straight lines

Discuss what is happening in the picture.

Trace the dotted lines. Color the picture.

©1993 Instructional Fair, Inc.   6   IF0251 Getting Ready for Kdg.

Small Motor Skills   tracing straight lines

Discuss make-believe and real pigs.

Trace the dotted line from the pig to the mud puddle.

©1993 Instructional Fair, Inc.   7   IF0251 Getting Ready for Kdg.

Small Motor Skills   staying between lines

Discuss mass transit systems used in big cities.

Draw a line through the streets from the train to the skyscrapers.

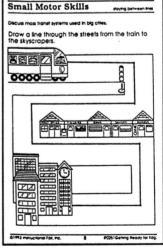

©1993 Instructional Fair, Inc.   8   IF0251 Getting Ready for Kdg.

Small Motor Skills
tracing curved lines

Discuss the child's favorite kinds of donuts.

Trace the dotted lines. Color the picture.

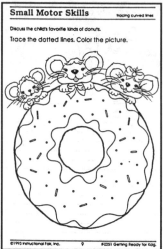

©1993 Instructional Fair, Inc.   9   IF0251 Getting Ready for Kdg.

Small Motor Skills
tracing curved lines

Discuss oceans.

Trace the dotted line from the starfish to the rock.

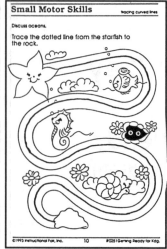

©1993 Instructional Fair, Inc.   10   IF0251 Getting Ready for Kdg.

Small Motor Skills
staying between lines

Discuss the picture.

Draw a line from the beaver to the dam following the path.

©1993 Instructional Fair, Inc.   11   IF0251 Getting Ready for Kdg.

Small Motor Skills
cutting and pasting

Use with page 13.
Discuss make-believe and real dogs.

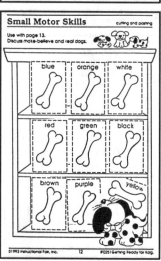

©1993 Instructional Fair, Inc.   12   IF0251 Getting Ready for Kdg.

Classifying
clothing

Discuss the pictures.

Draw a circle around the things that you can wear.

©1993 Instructional Fair, Inc.   15   IF0251 Getting Ready for Kdg.

Small Motor Skills
cutting and pasting

Use with page 17.
Discuss different types of cupcakes and how to make them.

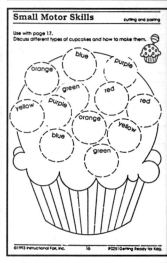

©1993 Instructional Fair, Inc.   16   IF0251 Getting Ready for Kdg.

Visual Discrimination
same

Discuss getting ready for bedtime. Have the child describe the three pictures in each row.

Color the two pictures in each row that are the same.

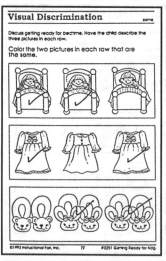

©1993 Instructional Fair, Inc.   19   IF0251 Getting Ready for Kdg.

Visual Discrimination
same

Discuss car racing.

Draw lines to match the cars that look the same.

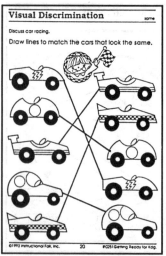

©1993 Instructional Fair, Inc.   20   IF0251 Getting Ready for Kdg.

Visual Discrimination
different

Discuss what you can put on crackers to make tasty snacks. Have the child describe the three pictures in each row.

Color the cracker in each row that is different.

©1993 Instructional Fair, Inc.   21   IF0251 Getting Ready for Kdg.

©1993 Instructional Fair, Inc.   IF0251 Getting Ready for Kdg.

Visual Discrimination
small motor skills

Use with page 23.
Discuss favorite zoo animals.

Cut out the puzzle pieces on page 24. Paste them where they belong in the puzzle frame. Color the picture.

Visual Discrimination
different

Discuss the toys in the top picture.

Find and circle 8 things in the top picture that are not in the bottom one.

Auditory Discrimination
same

Have the child name all of the pictures.

Draw lines to match the pictures that begin with the same sound.

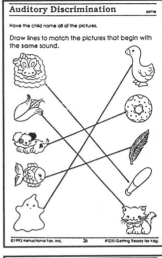

Auditory Discrimination
same

Have the child name all of the pictures.

Draw lines to match the pictures that begin with the same sound.

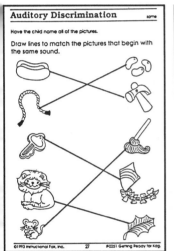

Auditory Discrimination
same

Have the child name all of the pictures.

Draw lines to match the pictures that begin with the same sound.

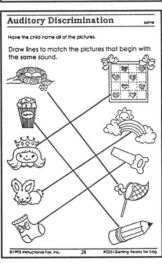

Auditory Discrimination
same

Have the child name all of the pictures.

Draw lines to match the pictures that begin with the same sound.

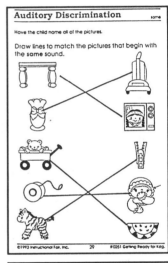

Reading Readiness
first

Have the child describe what is happening in each of the pictures.

Circle the pictures in each row that shows what happened first.

Reading Readiness
last

Have the child describe what is happening in each of the pictures.

Circle the picture in each row that shows what happened last.

Alphabet
capital letters

As you point to each letter, have the child name it.

Connect the puzzle dots in alphabetical order.
A B C D E F G H I J K L M N O P Q R S T U V W X Y Z

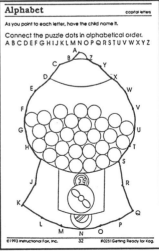

Alphabet
lower-case letters

As you point to each letter, have the child name it.

Connect the puzzle dots in alphabetical order.
a b c d e f g h i j k l m n o p q r s t u v w x y z

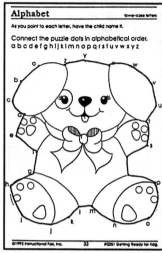

©1993 Instructional Fair, Inc. 33 IF0251 Getting Ready for Kdg.

Colors
red

Have the child name things that are red.

Color the spaces marked red with a red crayon.

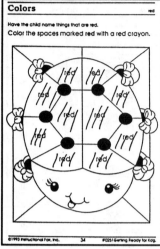

©1993 Instructional Fair, Inc. 34 IF0251 Getting Ready for Kdg.

Colors
blue

Have the child name the pictures and the color.

Draw a line from the crayon to the things that could be blue. Color the pictures.

©1993 Instructional Fair, Inc. 35 IF0251 Getting Ready for Kdg.

Colors
yellow

Have the child name the pictures and the colors.

Color the paintbrush and the three pictures that could be yellow.

©1993 Instructional Fair, Inc. 36 IF0251 Getting Ready for Kdg.

Colors
orange

Have the child name things that are orange.

Color the spaces marked orange with an orange crayon.

©1993 Instructional Fair, Inc. 37 IF0251 Getting Ready for Kdg.

Colors
green

Have the child name the pictures and the color.

Draw a line from the crayon to the things that could be green. Color the pictures.

©1993 Instructional Fair, Inc. 38 IF0251 Getting Ready for Kdg.

Colors
purple

Have the child name the pictures and the color.

Color the paintbrush and the three pictures that could be purple.

©1993 Instructional Fair, Inc. 39 IF0251 Getting Ready for Kdg.

Colors
black

Have the child name the pictures and the color.

Draw a line from the crayon to the things that could be black. Color the pictures.

©1993 Instructional Fair, Inc. 40 IF0251 Getting Ready for Kdg.

Colors
brown

Name things that are brown.

Color the spaces marked brown with a brown crayon.

©1993 Instructional Fair, Inc. 41 IF0251 Getting Ready for Kdg.

Colors

Have the child name the pictures and the color.

Color all the picture except the paintbrush and the three things that could be white.

©1993 Instructional Fair, Inc.   42   IF0251 Getting Ready for Kdg.

Colors

Have the child name the pictures and the color.

Draw a line from the crayon to the things that could be gray. Color the pictures.

©1993 Instructional Fair, Inc.   43   IF0251 Getting Ready for Kdg.

Colors

Name things that are pink.

Color the spaces marked pink with a pink crayon.

©1993 Instructional Fair, Inc.   44   IF0251 Getting Ready for Kdg.

Math

Draw the pictures to continue the pattern in each row.

©1993 Instructional Fair, Inc.   45   IF0251 Getting Ready for Kdg.

Math

Use with 47.

Cut out the pictures on page 47. Paste the pictures to continue the pattern in each row.

©1993 Instructional Fair, Inc.   46   IF0251 Getting Ready for Kdg.

Math

Color the first two monsters in each row the correct color. Color the remaining monsters in each row to continue the pattern.

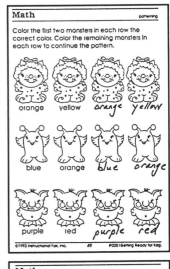

orange   yellow   *orange*   *yellow*

blue   orange   *blue*   *orange*

purple   red   *purple*   *red*

©1993 Instructional Fair, Inc.   49   IF0251 Getting Ready for Kdg.

Math

Color 1 glass of juice purple, 1 glass of juice orange, and 1 glass of juice red.

Practice writing the numeral 1.

©1993 Instructional Fair, Inc.   50   IF0251 Getting Ready for Kdg.

Math

Draw 2 smiling faces in each snapshot.

Practice writing the numeral 2.

2 2 2 2 2 2 2 2

©1993 Instructional Fair, Inc.   51   IF0251 Getting Ready for Kdg.

Math

Circle 3 things in each group. Color the pictures that are circled.

Practice writing the numeral 3.

3 3 3 3 3 3 3 3

©1993 Instructional Fair, Inc.   52   IF0251 Getting Ready for Kdg.

Math
count, recognize and write 4

Draw 4 letters in each mailbox.

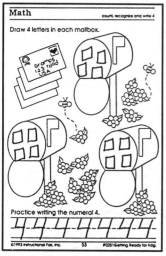

Practice writing the numeral 4.

4 4 4 4 4 4 4

Math
count, recognize and write 5

Color 5 scoops pink, 5 scoops brown, and leave 5 scoops white.

Practice writing the numeral 5.

5 5 5 5 5 5

Math
count and recognize 1 to 5

Count the number of objects and circle the correct numeral.

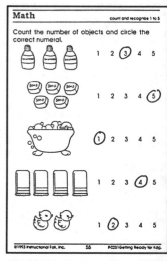

Math
count and write 1 to 5

Count the number of objects in each set. Write the correct numeral in the box.

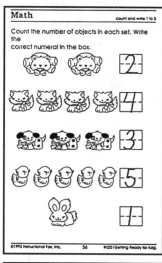

Math
sequence numbers 1 to 5

Count aloud from 1 to 5. Connect the dots in order from 1 to 5. Color the picture.

Shapes
circle

Trace the large circle. Color it red. Color the other the circles red.

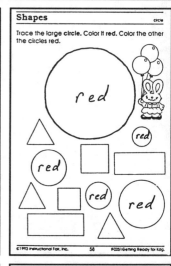

Shapes
square

Trace the large square. Color it yellow. Color the other squares yellow.

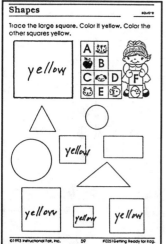

Shapes
triangle

Trace the large triangle. Color it blue. Color the other triangles blue.

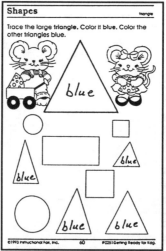

Shapes
rectangle

Trace the large rectangle. Color it green. Color the other rectangles green.

©1993 Instructional Fair, Inc.

IF0251 Getting Ready for Kdg.

School
behavior and courtesy

Discuss what is happening in each pair of pictures.

Draw a circle around the one picture in each pair that shows how you should behave. Color those pictures.

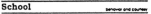

School
behavior and courtesy

Discuss what is happening in each pair of pictures.

Draw a circle around the one picture in each pair that shows how you should behave. Color those pictures.

Playground
safety and courtesy

Discuss what is happening in each pair of pictures.

Draw a circle around the one picture in each pair that shows a safe and courteous way to play on a playground.

Playground
safety and courtesy

Discuss what is happening in each pair of pictures.

Draw a circle around the one picture in each pair that shows a safe and courteous way to play on a playground.

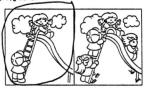

Listening & Following Directions

Use with page 66.

Listening & Following Directions

Use with page 68.

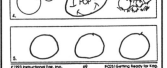

Listening & Following Directions

Read the directions aloud as the child completes the bottom of the page.

1. Draw a red X on the store where you can buy something for your feet.

2. Draw a purple circle around the store where you can buy food for a fish.

3. Draw an orange line under the store where you can buy something to play with.

4. Draw a yellow line over the store where you can buy a yummy dessert.

5. Draw a green car in front of the store where you can buy a new shirt for school.

6. Draw a blue X on the store where you can buy something to read.

Listening & Following Directions

Read the directions aloud as the child completes the bottom of the page.

1. Draw an X on the person who is in front of the line at the check-out counter.

2. Draw a circle around the person who is walking to the right.

3. Draw a hat on the cashier.

4. Design a sign over the produce section.

5. Draw a line under the last person in the line at the check-out counter.

6. Draw a line over the person who is walking to the left.

7. Color the picture.

Listening & Following Directions

Read the directions aloud as the child completes the bottom of the page.

1. Draw an X on the person who is under the tree.

2. Draw a circle around the horse that is inside the fence.

3. Color the grass on the hill green.

4. Color the pig that is climbing over the fence pink.

5. Color the horse that is next to the boy brown.

6. Draw a yellow X on the duck that is in the pond.

7. Color the picture.

©1993 Instructional Fair, Inc.　　　IF0251 Getting Ready for Kdg.

Colors

Have the child name things that are orange.

Color the spaces marked **orange** with an orange crayon.

Colors

Have the child name the pictures and the color.

Draw a line from the crayon to the things that could be **green**. Color the pictures.

Colors

Have the child name the pictures and the color.

Color the paintbrush and the three pictures that could be **purple**.

purple

Colors

Have the child name the pictures and the color.

Draw a line from the crayon to the things that could be **black**. Color the pictures.

©1993 Instructional Fair, Inc.

IF0251 Getting Ready for Kdg.

Colors

brown

Name things that are brown.

Color the spaces marked **brown** with a brown crayon.

Colors

Have the child name the pictures and the color.

Color all the picture except the paintbrush and the three things that could be **white**.

Colors

Have the child name the pictures and the color.

Draw a line from the crayon to the things that could be **gray**. Color the pictures.

Colors

Name things that are pink.

Color the spaces marked **pink** with a pink crayon

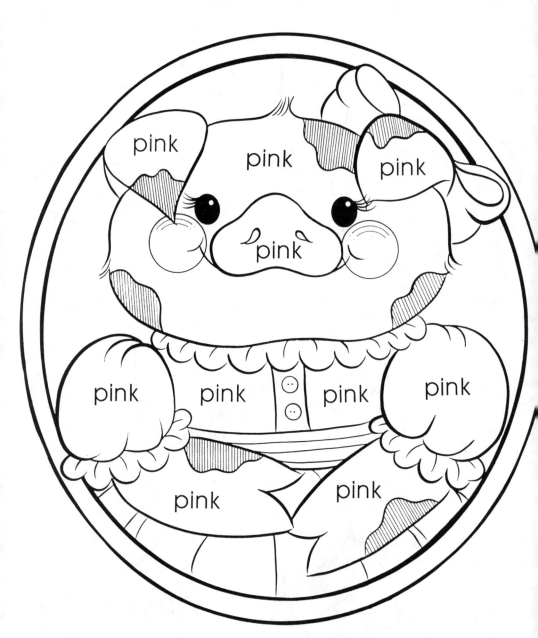

Math

Draw the pictures to continue the pattern in each row.

Math

Use with 47.

Cut out the pictures on page 47. Paste the pictures to continue the pattern in each row.

se with page 46.

Math

Color the first two monsters in each row the
correct color. Color the remaining monsters in
each row to continue the pattern.

orange   yellow

blue   orange

purple   red

Math

Color **1** glass of juice purple, **1** glass of juice orange, and **1** glass of juice red.

Juice 10¢

Practice writing the numeral 1.

- -

Math

Draw **2** smiling faces in each snapshot.

Practice writing the numeral 2.

Math

Circle **3** things in each group. Color the picture that are circled.

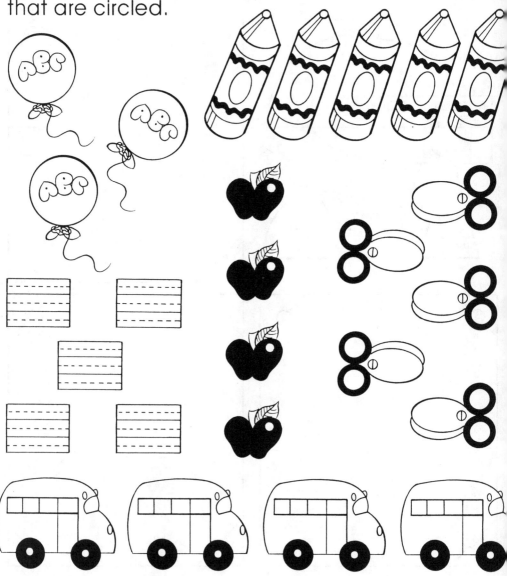

Practice writing the numeral 3.

- -

Draw **4** letters in each mailbox.

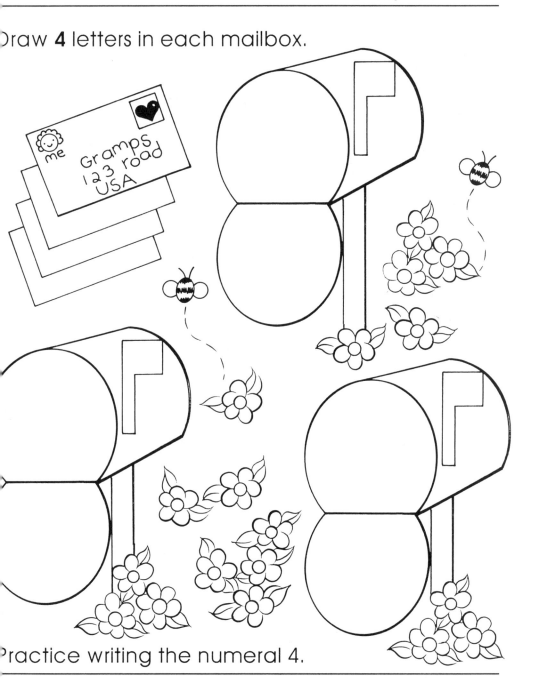

Practice writing the numeral 4.

Math

Color **5** scoops pink, **5** scoops brown, and leave **5** scoops white.

Practice writing the numeral 5.

_____

— — — — — — — — — — — — — — — — — —

_____

Count the number of objects and circle the correct numeral.

1   2   3   4   5

 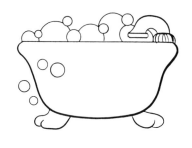

1   2   3   4   5

1   2   3   4   5

1   2   3   4   5

1   2   3   4   5

Math

Count the number of objects in each set. Write the correct numeral in the box.

Math

Count aloud from 1 to 5. Connect the dots in order from 1 to 5. Color the picture.

Shapes

Trace the large **circle.** Color it **red.** Color the other
the circles red.

Shapes

Trace the large **square.** Color it **yellow.** Color the other squares yellow.

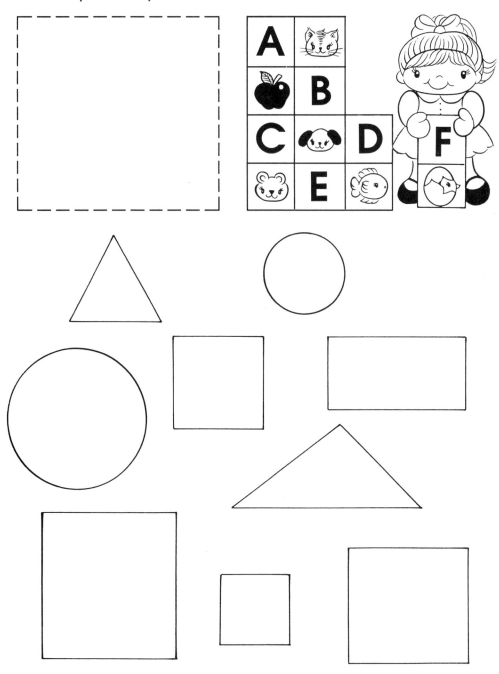

Shapes

Trace the large **triangle.** Color it **blue.** Color the other triangles blue.

Shapes

Trace the large **rectangle.** Color it **green.** Color the other rectangles green.

School

Discuss what is happening in each pair of pictures.

Draw a circle around the one picture in each pair that shows how you should behave. Color those pictures.

School

Discuss what is happening in each pair of pictures.

Draw a circle around the one picture in each pair that shows how you should behave. Color those pictures.

Playground

Discuss what is happening in each pair of pictures.

Draw a circle around the one picture in each pair that shows a safe and courteous way to play on a playground.

Playground

Discuss what is happening in each pair of pictures.

Draw a circle around the one picture in each pair that shows a safe and courteous way to play on a playground.

Listening & Following Directions

Use with page 67.

Read the story to the child. Then read the directions aloud as the child completes page 67.

A Super Day with Grandmother

Wow! Sue and Lee are very excited! Grandmother is taking them to the park for the entire day.

When they arrive at the park, Sue and Lee first run to the swings. Then they go up and down on the teeter-totter.

It's lunchtime already! Grandmother has packed the picnic basket with sandwiches, tasty red apples, crunchy potato chips and for dessert – cake!

After lunch they all sit under a shady tree as Grandmother reads a book to them. Of course, it is one of their favorite stories.

Then it is time to go home. Sue and Lee give Grandmother a great big hug for sharing such a wonderful day with them.

Directions for Page 67.

1. Draw a circle around the picture that shows where Sue, Lee and Grandmother went.

2. Draw a box around the picture that shows what Sue and Lee played on first.

3. Color the pictures of the foods that Grandmother packed in the picnic basket.

4. Draw a circle around the picture that shows what they did after lunch.

5. Draw a picture showing how Sue and Lee let their Grandmother know that they had a good time.

Listening & Following Directions

Use with page 66.

1.

2.

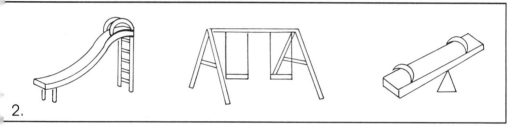

3.

4.

5.

Listening & Following Directions

Use with page 69.

Read the story to the child. Then read the directions aloud as you child completes page 69.

Bubbles

Do you like to make bubbles? Margo does! It is so easy. First she opens the jar of bubble soap. Then she carefully dips the bubble maker into the soap. After the soap covers the bubble maker, Margo pulls it out of the jar Then she waves the bubble maker in the air. Lots and lots of bubbles float up into the sky. When the sunlight shines through the soapy bubbles, it makes them appear to be many different colors. Blue bubbles, green bubbles and even pink bubbles! Look quickly! They're popping! Bu that's all right. Margo can make many, many more bubbles

Directions for Page 69.

1. Draw a box around the picture that shows what Margo likes to do.

2. Draw a circle around the picture that shows what Margo does first.

3. Color the bubbles the same colors as the ones in the story.

4. Draw a circle around the picture that shows how the bubbles disappear.

5. Draw three bubbles. Color them.

Listening & Following Directions

Use with page 68.

1.

2.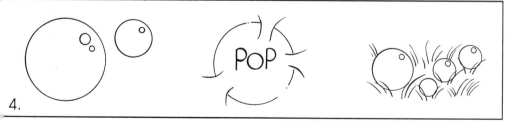

3.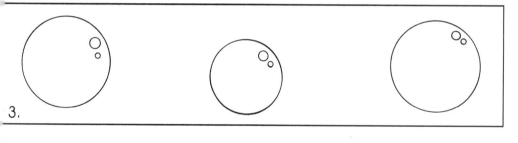

4.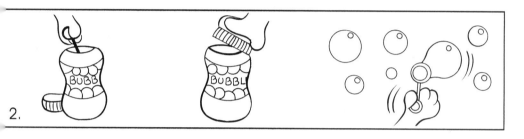

5.

Listening & Following Directions

Read the directions aloud as the child completes the bottom of the page.

1. Draw a red X **on** the store where you can buy something for your feet.

2. Draw a purple circle **around** the store where you can buy food for a fish.

3. Draw an orange line **under** the store where you can buy something to play with.

4. Draw a yellow line **over** the store where you can buy a yummy dessert.

5. Draw a green car **in front** of the store where you can buy a new shirt for school.

6. Draw a Blue X **on** the store where you can buy something to read.

Listening & Following Directions

Read the directions aloud as the child completes the bottom of the page.

1. Draw an X on the person who is **in front** of the line at the check-out counter.

2. Draw a circle around the person who is walking to the **right.**

3. Draw a hat **on** the cashier.

4. Design a sign **over** the produce section.

5. Draw a line **under** the last person in the line at the check-out counter.

6. Draw a line over the person who is walking to the **left.**

7. Color the picture.

Listening & Following Directions

Read the directions aloud as the child completes the bottom of the page.

1. Draw an X on the person who is **under** the tree.

2. Draw a circle around the horse that is **inside** the fence.

3. Color the grass **on** the hill green.

4. Color the pig that is climbing **over** the fence pink.

5. Color the horse that is **next to** the boy brown.

6. Draw a yellow X on the duck that is **in** the pond.

7. Color the picture.

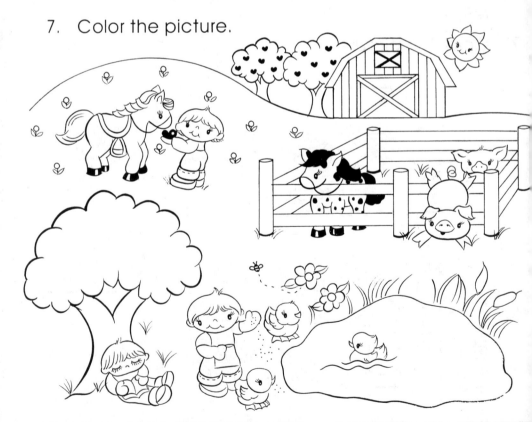